Woodrow Wilson

History Maker Bios

Laura Hamilton Waxman

⌐ LERNER PUBLICATIONS COMPANY • MINNEAPOLIS

Illustrations by Tim Parlin

Lerner Publications Company
A division of Lerner Publishing Group
241 First Avenue North
Minneapolis, Minnesota 55401 U.S.A.

Website address: www.lernerbooks.com

Library of Congress Cataloging-in-Publication Data

Waxman, Laura Hamilton.
    Woodrow Wilson / by Laura Hamilton Waxman.
        p.   cm. — (History maker bios)
    Includes bibliographical references and index.
    ISBN-13: 978–0–8225–6053–1 (lib. bdg. : alk. paper)
    ISBN-10: 0–8225–6053–4 (lib. bdg. : alk. paper)
        1. Wilson, Woodrow, 1856–1924—Juvenile literature. 2. Presidents—United States—Biography—Juvenile literature. I. Title. II. Series.
    E767.W38 2006
    973.91'3092—dc22 [B]   2005032396

Manufactured in the United States of America
1 2 3 4 5 6 – JR – 11 10 09 08 07 06

TABLE OF CONTENTS

Introduction

As a young man, Woodrow Wilson dreamed of becoming a great leader. He believed the best leaders made life better for people. In 1912, Wilson ran for president of the United States and won. As president, he helped improve life for many Americans.

In 1914, Wilson turned his attention to the people of the world. That year, World War I broke out in Europe. Wilson saw that the war caused great suffering. He worked hard to bring about a lasting peace. Wilson dreamed of a day when countries would stop fighting wars altogether. He dreamed of a world where everyone lived in peace and freedom.

This is his story.

TOMMY WILSON

Thomas Woodrow Wilson was born in his family's big white house near midnight on December 28, 1856. Jessie Woodrow Wilson and Joseph Wilson called their first son Tommy. They had high hopes for him and cared for his every need.

Before he was born Tommy's parents had moved from the northern part of the country to the southern part. They lived in Staunton, Virginia.

In 1858 they moved once again to Augusta, Georgia. Tommy was only four years old when war began between the North and the South. This war became known as the Civil War (1861–1865).

The North and the South disagreed for many reasons. Slavery was one of the reasons that they fought. The Northern states had outlawed slavery years earlier. Many Northerners wanted to end slavery in the Southern states too. But Southerners believed they needed the work of slaves to keep their farms and plantations running smoothly. The South lost the war. In 1865, the United States outlawed slavery.

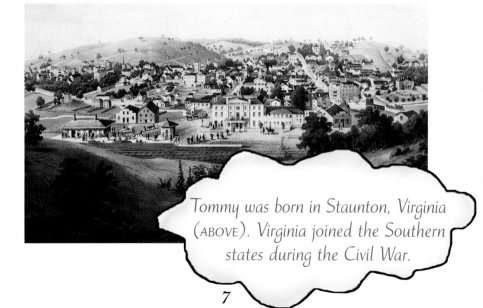

Tommy was born in Staunton, Virginia (ABOVE). Virginia joined the Southern states during the Civil War.

Richmond, Virginia, was one of the cities badly damaged during the Civil War.

By then, many Southern cities had been destroyed by the fighting. And many families had lost fathers, sons, and brothers in battle. Tommy had learned an important lesson. War caused terrible pain and suffering.

Tommy's father taught his son other lessons about life. Joseph Wilson was a Christian minister. Each Sunday morning, Tommy and his family sat in the fourth row of his father's church. There they listened to Joseph Wilson give sermons, or religious speeches. Joseph was a powerful speaker. Tommy saw that people respected him.

After church, Tommy often spent hours studying with his father. Joseph taught his son about books, science, and religion. He also taught Tommy to set high goals for himself. Joseph believed it was a man's duty to make the world a better place. He expected Tommy to meet that challenge when he grew up.

Tommy liked studying with his father. But he was not a good student at school. He could not read or write until he was around twelve years old. Tommy also did not make friends easily. He was tall, skinny, and shy.

Tommy liked spending time with his father, Joseph Wilson (RIGHT).

When Tommy was sixteen years old, he went to Davidson College in North Carolina. His father expected him to become a minister. Tommy spent only one year at Davidson. In 1875, he switched to the College of New Jersey, which became known as Princeton University.

Tommy loved his new school. For the first time, he made good friends. They talked about history, politics, and religion. Tommy and his friends even began a debate club. There Tommy learned to be a powerful speaker like his father.

This portrait of Tommy was taken when he was seventeen years old.

READING AND WRITING

Many people have wondered why Woodrow Wilson took longer than most children to learn to read and write. He may have had dyslexia. Dyslexia is a kind of learning disability. Having dyslexia does not make a person less smart. But it does make reading and writing difficult. Woodrow found ways to overcome these problems. For example, he learned a simple kind of writing called shorthand.

Tommy soon realized that he did not want to be a minister. Instead, he dreamed of becoming a leader. Tommy and a college friend made a promise to each other. They vowed that they would learn all they could about being good leaders. They would also learn about the best ways to run a government. Then, one day, they could use their knowledge to make the world a better place.

2 POPULAR PROFESSOR

Tommy graduated from Princeton University in the spring of 1879. He next went to school to become a lawyer. He also decided to change his name. He would try using his middle name. The name Woodrow suited him. But being a lawyer didn't. He worked as a lawyer for only a year. After that, he chose to return to school and study history and politics.

Woodrow's studies were not the only thing on his mind. He thought an awful lot about Ellen Axson too. Ellen was the daughter of a minister back home in Georgia. She was a bright-eyed and intelligent young woman. She was also a talented artist who had won prizes for her paintings.

Woodrow married Ellen on June 24, 1885. That same summer, he finished his studies for a Ph.D. at Johns Hopkins University in Baltimore, Maryland.

Woodrow met Ellen Axson (RIGHT) in 1883. They were married two years later.

Woodrow may have still dreamed of becoming a leader. But his first job was as a professor at Bryn Mawr College in Pennsylvania. A few years later, he got a new job teaching at Wesleyan University in Connecticut.

The students at both schools loved Woodrow's classes. The tall professor with blue gray eyes excited students with new ideas about government and politics. Along with teaching, Woodrow wrote about and published his ideas.

WOODROW INSIDE AND OUT

Woodrow was shy all his life. To strangers he seemed stiff and distant. Someone once compared him to a cold fish! But with friends and family, he could be quite different. Woodrow cared deeply for his wife and children. In letters to Ellen, he often wrote of his great love for her. And Ellen's love was very important to him. Her kindness and support kept him going through hard times.

Woodrow enjoyed spending time with his daughters, Jessie, Margaret, and Eleanor (LEFT TO RIGHT).

Life at the Wilson home was also busy. By 1889, Ellen had given birth to three daughters. Woodrow loved to spend his evenings with Margaret, Jessie, and Eleanor. He read to them from his favorite books, sang, and played games with them.

In 1890, Woodrow returned to Princeton University in New Jersey. This time, he arrived as an experienced professor. At Princeton, Woodrow's classes were more popular than ever. Year after year, students voted for him as their favorite teacher.

Woodrow was named president of Princeton University in 1902.

At the same time, people around the country were also taking notice of the popular Princeton professor. Woodrow Wilson had published books and articles about his ideas for government. He also gave speeches around the country.

When Woodrow was forty-five years old, he became president of Princeton. He took his new job as a leader seriously. He planned to make big changes. Many of the professors and leaders at Princeton liked their bold new leader.

One morning in May 1906, Woodrow woke up blind in his left eye. He and Ellen visited some doctors. The doctors told him that he had suffered from a stroke. Strokes can harm the brain, and they can also be deadly. The doctors said that Woodrow needed to rest. If he didn't get better, he might have to stop working completely.

It was terrible news for Woodrow. But he tried to do what was best for his health. He and his family went on a long summer vacation to Great Britain.

Big Ben is a famous clock tower in Great Britain, where Woodrow spent the summer with his family.

In Great Britain, Woodrow took long walks and relaxed. His eyesight returned, and his health improved. He knew he might have another stroke if he worked too hard. But he decided to return to his job at Princeton that fall.

Woodrow still wanted to make changes to the university. But not everyone there still agreed with him. Woodrow was stubborn. He ignored those who disagreed with him and pushed forward with his ideas. That made many people angry. Some of them wanted a new president.

By 1910, Woodrow was ready to leave Princeton University. He thought about his old dream to be a leader in the government. Somehow, he told himself, he would make that dream come true.

3 FAMOUS GOVERNOR

In the summer of 1910, Woodrow Wilson had some good luck. Members of New Jersey's Democratic political party came to him with a question. Did he want to become the state's governor? First, he would have to win an election against a member of the Republican Party. Candidates from the Democratic and Republican parties competed in elections throughout the country.

While running for governor, Wilson shakes hands with supporters.

Wilson agreed to run for governor of New Jersey. To win, he had to convince voters to choose him. He spent that fall traveling around the state giving speeches.

Woodrow Wilson said he would work hard to make New Jersey a better place. He believed that the rich had too much political power. Too many people lived in poverty. He thought the government should help working people improve their lives. Voters liked what Wilson said.

Wilson won the election that fall. He became governor in January 1911. As the state's leader, he worked with the state's lawmakers. Together they passed new laws to protect New Jersey's citizens.

One new law said that businesses must give money to workers who get hurt on the job. Another law kept the prices of public utilities from going too high. Public utilities are services that citizens use every day. The utilities in Wilson's state included transportation such as trains and trolleys. They also included electricity and telephone services.

In the early 1900s, many people got around town on trolleys.

Wilson's work as governor made him well known around the country. By 1912, Democrats began to wonder if he might run for president of the United States. Wilson was proud of his work as New Jersey's governor. But he believed he could do even more as the country's leader.

In June, the Democratic Party chose Woodrow Wilson to be their candidate for president. The news spread quickly to his hometown. Soon a cheering crowd and a brass band arrived at his house to celebrate. The Wilson family was amazed to see how popular he had become.

Many people went to Wilson's home to show their support for him as a presidential candidate.

The president at the time was a Republican named William Howard Taft. Taft was running for reelection as president. In order to win, Wilson would have to get more votes than Taft.

Wilson also needed to beat a third candidate, the famous Theodore Roosevelt. Roosevelt had been a popular president from 1901 to 1909. In 1912, he created a new political party and decided to run for president again.

TEDDY ROOSEVELT

Theodore Roosevelt, called Teddy, was the opposite of Woodrow Wilson in many ways. Woodrow was tall and thin. Theodore was strong and muscular. Woodrow was private and shy. Teddy was loud and talkative. Woodrow liked playing tennis and taking quiet walks. Teddy Roosevelt loved hunting and adventuring in the wilderness. But both men shared a love of reading and wrote books of their own.

Wilson talks to a crowd, explaining why he should be the next president of the United States.

Wilson traveled all over the country making speeches. He excited people with his bold plan for the country. He called his plan the New Freedom. Large crowds squeezed into buildings, baseball parks, and racetracks to hear him. One day in New York City, the crowd cheered for an hour before Wilson spoke a single word.

Wilson said that too many people lived in poverty. He believed that the owners of big businesses charged high prices for important goods and services. They made it difficult for new business owners to succeed. Wilson promised that his New Freedom plan would be fairer to all Americans.

Many voters believed him. On Election Day in 1912, they voted for Woodrow Wilson to become the next president of the United States.

A crowd gathered at the nation's capital to watch Wilson take the oath of office.

4 PRESIDENT WILSON

A month after Wilson became president, he decided to give a speech in front of the U.S. Congress. Wilson was the first president to speak to all of the country's representatives in more than one hundred years. In his speech, Wilson talked about the problem of high tariffs.

Tariffs are a kind of tax—money paid to the government by a person or a business. The U.S. government had been charging high tariffs on goods coming from other countries. This made foreign goods very expensive. U.S. business owners charged a little less for their goods than foreign businesses. But they still charged high prices.

Under Wilson's leadership, Congress passed a law to lower tariffs. Many goods from foreign countries became more affordable. That caused U.S. business owners to lower their prices too.

Woodrow Wilson makes a speech to Congress.

Wilson continued to work with Congress to pass other important laws. One law created the Federal Reserve System. The Federal Reserve makes sure banks are running smoothly and fairly. It also helps keep the U.S. economy healthy and strong.

Another law created the Federal Trade Commission. This government agency keeps watch over large businesses. It helps to make sure businesses do not charge unfair prices.

MONOPOLIES

In Wilson's lifetime, some wealthy business owners had monopolies. To have a monopoly, a business owner buys other businesses that sell the same goods, such as steel or oil. Then the business owner does not have to compete with anyone else for customers. He or she can control the prices the customers pay for the goods. Woodrow Wilson and the Federal Trade Commission made it hard for business owners to have monopolies.

In the early 1900s, many children worked in mines and factories. These boys are working in a glass factory.

Wilson also helped pass laws to protect workers. One law said that factories could no longer hire young children. Until then, children had worked long hours in dangerous places. Another law said that railroad companies could not make their employees work more than eight hours in one day.

Cars like this 1913 Chevrolet were just becoming popular when Wilson was president.

Wilson's work kept him busy. Most mornings, he worked in his office in the White House. He also met with leaders from the United States and other nations. He spent lunchtime with his wife and daughters. After lunch, he went back to his office to work. Before dinner, he tried to relax so he could stay healthy. He often played a game of golf or went for a ride in a new invention—the automobile.

In the summer of 1914, Wilson learned that war had broken out in Europe. This war became known as World War I (1914–1918). France and Britain wanted the United States to help them beat Germany.

Wilson refused to get the United States involved in the war. He still had terrible memories of the Civil War. He did not want U.S. soldiers to die fighting.

German U-boats attacked many merchant ships and passenger ships during World War I.

Wilson had another problem of his own. His wife Ellen was ill with a kidney disease. For weeks she lay in bed too weak to move. Wilson sat by her side hour after hour. He hoped she would get well. But Ellen died on August 6, 1914.

Wilson missed Ellen deeply. He even wondered if he should be president any longer. He said he was too sad to run the country. Wilson's friends tried to comfort him.

This portrait of Ellen Wilson was taken in 1912.

Wilson found happiness with his new wife, Edith.

One day in February 1915, Wilson met a woman named Edith Bolling Galt. Edith made him smile and laugh. He felt happy for the first time in months. He quickly fell in love. Wilson married Edith on December 18 of that same year. With Edith by his side, Wilson felt strong again.

In 1916, Wilson won reelection as president. That same year, he began thinking more about the war in Europe. He began to have a new dream. He wanted to bring about a lasting, worldwide peace.

5 PEACEMAKER

Wilson knew that most wars ended when one side lost. But the anger caused by the war often stayed with both sides. That meant the two sides might fight another war in the future.

Wilson wanted to end the war in Europe before any country lost or won. If both sides chose peace together, then the peace might last. Wilson called this a "fair peace." He believed it would permanently end war in Europe.

Wilson shared his ideas with the leaders of France and Britain and with the leaders of Germany. But they were not interested in ending the war. Both sides believed they could win.

Wilson still hoped to keep the United States out of the war. But in March 1917, Germany sank three U.S. ships near Great Britain. Wilson also learned that Germany was trying to get Mexico to make war on the United States. Wilson realized the United States could not avoid the war any longer. The country joined Great Britain and France and entered the war in April 1917.

U.S. soldiers fight against the German army.

Wilson had not given up on his dreams for peace, however. He set up secret meetings to plan for the end of the war. The meetings led to a list of ideas for creating a fair peace. Wilson called this list the Fourteen Points. His ideas were translated into many different languages. People all over the world read about them.

Wilson cared most deeply about the last idea on the list. He wanted to create a league, or an organization, of nations. This league of countries would work together to stop new wars from starting.

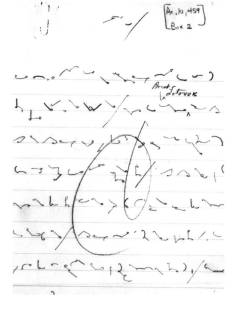

Wilson made notes for his Fourteen Points in shorthand.

WORLD WAR I

In Wilson's time, World War I was known as the Great War. Never before had a single war included so many countries. Europeans hoped the war would end by Christmas 1914. Instead, it went on for four long years. During that time, the war spread to many countries. Even men from faraway places such as Africa and Australia took part in the fighting. In all, nine million soldiers lost their lives.

With the help of the United States, Britain and France won the war against Germany near the end of 1918. The time for peace had come at last. The leaders of Europe planned to gather in Paris, France, to work out a peace treaty, or agreement.

Wilson traveled with Edith to Paris. There he was met by a large crowd of people. To them, President Wilson was a hero. He had given people hope for an end to all war.

Wilson worked from winter to early summer with the leaders of Europe on an important treaty. It was called the Treaty of Versailles. In June 1919, the leaders finally agreed on a plan for peace. The Treaty of Versailles included a plan to create the League of Nations. The league would include leaders from many different countries, including the United States.

The Treaty of Versailles was signed at the Palace of Versailles in France.

Edith was with Woodrow Wilson while he was in Paris.

Some leaders of Europe stayed in Paris to work out more peace treaties. Wilson returned home. He was hopeful about the world's future. But not everyone in the United States shared his feelings.

Many Republican lawmakers in Washington, D.C., disliked the idea of joining the League of Nations. The United States had stayed out of other countries' problems in the past. They believed the United States should continue its policy. These lawmakers said they would vote against U.S. membership in the league.

Wilson traveled the country by train.

Wilson was ready to fight for his dream of peace. He planned to give speeches all over the United States about the League of Nations. Edith wanted him to stay home, though. She thought he needed time to rest and get stronger. But Wilson was determined.

During the fall of 1919, Wilson and his wife took a train across the United States. He gave speech after speech. Wilson said that the League of Nations would give the world a peace never dreamed of before. Without the league, Wilson believed, another great war was sure to take place.

Wilson inspired Americans with his dream of world peace. They came to believe that the League of Nations was a good idea. But Wilson used up his strength giving speeches, and he became very ill. He ended the trip early and returned to the White House, but it was too late.

On October 2, 1919, Wilson had a terrible stroke. He could not move the left side of his body. He also could not think or speak clearly. Without his leadership, Congress voted against joining the League of Nations.

Wilson did not fully recover from his stroke, but he still made some public appearances.

The Nobel Peace Prize is awarded for outstanding work toward international peace.

Despite Congress's vote against the league, Wilson's belief in the organization impressed people in other parts of the world. In December 1920, a committee in Norway awarded Wilson the 1919 Nobel Peace Prize. The Nobel Peace Prize is given out only once each year. It honors some of the world's greatest peacemakers. As a result of his stroke, however, Wilson was unable to travel to Norway to accept the prize in person.

Wilson was ill for the rest of his presidency. Edith cared for him. She also became his voice in the White House. She met with government leaders and representatives on his behalf.

Wilson's presidency ended in early 1921. He died three years later, on February 3, 1924. Although Wilson's League of Nations did not prevent another world war, his ideas live on. Wilson believed the United States should not stand back from the problems of other countries. He believed U.S. leaders should help bring peace and freedom to people around the world. His ideas helped shape the world we know.

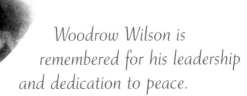

Woodrow Wilson is remembered for his leadership and dedication to peace.

TIMELINE

WOODROW WILSON WAS BORN ON DECEMBER 28, 1856.

In the year . . .

1858 Woodrow moved to Augusta, Georgia.

1875 he went to College of New Jersey.

1879 he began studying law.

1883 he went to Johns Hopkins University.

1885 he graduated from Johns Hopkins. `Age 28`
he married Ellen Axson on June 24.
he got a job teaching at Bryn Mawr College.

1886 his first daughter, Margaret, was born.

1887 his second daughter, Jessie, was born.

1888 he began teaching at Wesleyan University.

1889 his third daughter, Eleanor, was born.

1890 he returned to Princeton as a professor.

1902 he was elected president of Princeton.

1906 he had a stroke.

1910 he was elected governor of New Jersey.

1912 he won the election for U.S. president. `Age 55`

1914 World War I began.
Ellen died.

1915 he married Edith Bolling Galt.

1916 he won a second term as president.

1917 the United States joined the war.

1918 World War I ended.

1919 he met with European leaders in Paris.
he traveled across the United States.
he had another stroke on October 2.

1920 he won the 1919 Nobel Peace Prize. `Age 63`

1921 his eight years as president ended.

1924 he died on February 3. `Age 67`

44

WOODROW WILSON'S DREAM

Woodrow Wilson had said that Europe would have another war without a League of Nations. The league was created, but the world's leaders could not keep another world war from happening. In 1939, World War II began. Once again, France and Britain were fighting against Germany. Other nations also took part in the fighting. The United States entered the war in 1941. Together, the United States, France, Britain, and Russia defeated Germany and Japan in 1945.

After the war, leaders remembered Wilson's dream of a fair and lasting peace. In October 1945, fifty countries came together to form a new league. This time they called it the United Nations, or the UN. Over the years, nearly two hundred countries have joined the UN. The UN works to bring peace to countries at war. UN food and medical programs make life better for men, women, and children around the world.

The United Nations' headquarters are in New York City.

45

FURTHER READING

Ashby, Ruth. *Woodrow and Edith Wilson.* Milwaukee: World Almanac Library, 2005. This book provides information about President Woodrow Wilson and First Lady Edith Wilson.

Brezina, Corona. *The Treaty of Versailles, 1919.* New York: Rosen Publishing, 2005. This book explains the peace settlement that was signed after World War I.

Holden, Henry M. *Woodrow Wilson.* Berkeley Heights, NJ: Enslow, 2003. This biography provides more information on U.S. president Woodrow Wilson.

Swain, Gwenyth. *Theodore Roosevelt.* Minneapolis: Lerner Publications Company, 2005. This biography reviews the life and career of Theodore Roosevelt, twenty-sixth president of the United States.

WEBSITES

American Experience: Woodrow Wilson
http://www.pbs.org/wgbh/amex/wilson/
Learn more about Woodrow Wilson's life and career, and see many photographs of the president.

Biography of Woodrow Wilson
http://www.whitehouse.gov/history/presidents/ww28.html
Read about President Wilson on the official White House website.

The Great War and the Shaping of the 20th Century
http://www.pbs.org/greatwar/
Learn all about World War I through text, timelines, maps, and photographs.

The United Nations
http://www.un.org/
Read about the United Nations on its official website.

SELECT BIBLIOGRAPHY

BOOKS
Auchincloss, Louis. *Woodrow Wilson*. New York: Viking Penguin, 2000.

Brands, H. W. *Woodrow Wilson*. New York: Times Books, 2003.

Clements, Kendrick A. *The Presidency of Woodrow Wilson*. Lawrence: University Press of Kansas, 1992.

Clements, Kendrick A. *Woodrow Wilson: World's Statesman*. Boston: Twayne Publishers, 1987.

Heckscher, August. *Woodrow Wilson: A Biography*. New York: Charles Scribner's Sons, 1991.

MacMillan, Margaret. *Paris 1919: Six Months That Changed the World*. New York: Random House, 2002.

Walworth, Arthur. *Woodrow Wilson: American Prophet*. New York: Longmans, Green and Co., 1958.

Wilson, Edith Bolling Galt. *My Memoir*. New York: Bobbs-Merrill Company, 1939.

VIDEO
American Experience: Woodrow Wilson. WGBH Educational Foundation and Community Television of Southern California, 2001.

INDEX

Acknowledgments

The images in this book are used with the permission of: © Stock Montage/ Hulton Archive/Getty Images, p. 4; Library of Congress, pp. 7 (LC-USZC4-1888), 10 (LC-USZ62-100488), 17 (pan for geog-England no. 6), 20 (LC-USZ62-92465), 22 (PAN SUBJECT – Groups, no. 127), 25 (LC-USZ62-107685), 29 (LC-DIG-nclc-01151), 31 (LC-USZ62-075818), 32 (LC-USZ62-100079), 33 (LC-USZ62-21328), 36 (LC-MSS-46029-14), 43 (LC-USZ62-085704); © North Wind Picture Archives, p. 8; Woodrow Wilson Collection. Public Policy Papers. Department of Rare Books and Special Collections. Princeton University Library. pp. 9, 13, 15 (left), 16, 24, 40; Ray Stannard Baker Papers. Public Policy Papers. Department of Rare Books and Special Collections. Princeton University Library. p. 15 (right); © Wallace G. Levison/Time Life Pictures/Getty Images, p. 21; National Archives, pp. 27 (W&C 428), 35 (W&C 620); General Motors, p. 30; © A. A. M. Van der Heyden/ Independent Picture Service, p. 38; © Hulton Archive/Getty Images, p. 39; © Brown Brothers, p. 41; UN/DPI Photo, p. 42; © Les Stone/Zuma Press, p. 45.

Front Cover: Library of Congress (LC-USZ62-6247). Back Cover: UN/DPI Photo.